Remembering

Salt Lake City

Jeff Burbank

TURNER
PUBLISHING COMPANY

T0169586

This 1950 photo, taken from the apex of the City and County Building (451 South State Street), shows how the development of downtown Salt Lake City had progressed, with some newer buildings including the University of Utah and Judge Mercy Hospital.

Remembering

Salt Lake
City

Turner Publishing Company
4507 Charlotte Avenue • Suite 100
Nashville, Tennessee 37209
(615) 255-2665

Remembering Salt Lake City

www.turnerpublishing.com

Library of Congress Control Number: 2010924322

ISBN: 978-1-59652-665-5

Printed in the United States of America

ISBN: 978-1-68336-881-6 (pbk)

10 11 12 13 14 15 16—0 9 8 7 6 5 4 3 2 1

CONTENTS

ACKNOWLEDGMENTS.. VII

PREFACE VIII

FROM MORMON ENCLAVE TO AMERICAN CITY
(1880–1905) 1

NEW BUILDINGS, NEW STREETS, NEW FACES
(1906–1919) 27

STALLED BY THE GREAT DEPRESSION
(1920–1939) 109

SUBURBAN GROWTH AND PRESIDENTIAL VISITS
(1940–1950s) 123

NOTES ON THE PHOTOGRAPHS 131

Civil War veterans from Utah pose on the ornate porch of a Salt Lake City home in 1888.

Acknowledgments

This volume, *Remembering Salt Lake City,* is the result of the cooperation and efforts of many individuals and organizations. It is with great thanks that we acknowledge the valuable contribution of the following for their generous support:

Library of Congress

National Archives

Special Collections Department, J. Willard Marriott Library, University of Utah

Utah State Historical Society

PREFACE

The founding of Salt Lake City continued a tradition dating back to colonial America, as a group of pilgrims sought to establish a place where members of their religion would be free from persecution for their beliefs. The first settlers in the Salt Lake Valley envisioned a planned community where religion, government, and commerce would intermingle. As new residents, practicing other religions, arrived, the role of the Church of Jesus Christ of Latter-day Saints—sometimes simply called "the Church"—was diminished in government and commerce, and the city became more heterogeneous. Regardless, it still holds a unique place among American cities.

Thousands of historic photographs of this shining city near the Great Salt Lake reside in local and national archives. This book began with the observation that, while those photographs are of great interest to many, they are not easily accessible. It seeks to provide easy access to a valuable, objective look into the history of Salt Lake City, for residents and visitors alike.

The power of photographs is that they are less subjective than words in their treatment of history. Although the photographer can make subjective decisions regarding subject matter and how to capture and present it, photographs seldom interpret the past to the extent textual histories can. For this reason, photography is uniquely positioned to offer an original, untainted look at the past, allowing the viewer to learn for himself what the world was like a century or more ago.

This project represents countless hours of review and research. The researchers and writer have reviewed thousands of photographs in numerous archives. We greatly appreciate the generous assistance of the individuals and organizations listed in the acknowledgments of this work, without whom this project could not have been completed.

The goal in publishing this work is to provide broader access to this set of extraordinary photographs that seek to inspire, provide perspective, and evoke insight that might assist people who are responsible for determining Salt Lake City's future. In addition, the book seeks to preserve the past with adequate respect and reverence.

With the exception of touching up imperfections that have accrued with the passage of time and cropping where necessary, no changes have been made. The focus and clarity of many images are limited to the technology and the ability of the photographer at the time they were recorded.

The work is divided into eras, beginning with the 1880s and concluding in the 1950s. In each of these sections we have made an effort to capture various aspects of life through our selection of photographs. People, commerce, transportation, infrastructure, religious institutions, and educational institutions have been included to provide a broad perspective.

We encourage readers to reflect as they go walking in Salt Lake City, strolling its broad thoroughfares, its parks, and its neighborhoods. It is the publisher's hope that in utilizing this work, longtime residents will learn something new and that new residents will gain a perspective on where the city has been, so that each can contribute to its future.

This wide shot of downtown Salt Lake City, taken from the roof of the City and County Building on May 27, 1920, shows a maturing town. Buildings pictured here include the Walker Brothers Bank Building, First Security Bank Building, Deseret National Bank Building, Hotel Utah, the Joseph Smith Memorial Building, and the Utah State Capitol. Evidence of changing times is visible—Fuller Auto Works stands next to the Utah Livery Stable, and motor vehicles are parked behind Coombs & Hagen's carriage shop in the center foreground.

From Mormon Enclave to American City

(1880–1905)

Horse-drawn vehicles line up in downtown Salt Lake City in the early 1880s, outside a wagon factory, Studebaker Brothers Manufacturing. The Midwest-based Studebaker company developed a national reputation for building sturdy wagons, popular for use in mining. In 1902, it would begin producing automobiles.

The outside of the Zion's Cooperative Mercantile Institution as it looked on Main Street in the late 1880s. By then, much of downtown Salt Lake City had been planned and developed with municipal and commercial buildings. Sanitation was one problem that remained. Dead work animals and garbage piled up along city streets, and the area lacked a sewer system until the 1890s.

Railroad service to Salt Lake City was well established by the late 1870s, as seen by this photograph of the Denver and Rio Grande Railroad Station about 1880. The nation's rails were joined at Promontory Summit, Utah, on May 10, 1869, but the Union Pacific Railroad's route bypassed Salt Lake City in favor of Ogden. The Utah Central Railroad, owned by the Church of Latter-day Saints, was connected to the Union Pacific line in 1870. With 15,000 people watching, Brigham Young himself pounded in the last spike, which linked Salt Lake City with the rest of the United States by rail.

An engineer looks out the window of the engine of a train stopped at the Denver and Rio Grande Depot about 1880. The railroad shipped ore, including silver, copper, lead, and coal, from area mines in places like Bingham and Park City to Salt Lake City for smelting and processing. The city became a mining capital in the region, greatly expanding its economy and the ethnic diversity of its population.

Not long after establishing the Zion's Cooperative Mercantile Institution's main building in 1868, dealing in clothing and dry goods, a second location opened that sold groceries, farm tools, stoves, and hardware.

A three-story decorative star in honor of Utah's statehood adorned the Dinwoodey Furniture building in 1896.

Laying the capstone of the Mormon Temple and Tabernacle in 1892.

A choir of men, dressed in dark clothing, and women wearing white pose inside the Mormon Tabernacle during statehood celebrations in 1896. The Church's choir would eventually achieve world renown. Brigham Young asked Joseph Harris Ridges, who grew up near an organ factory in England, to construct an organ for the Tabernacle. At various times, its bellows have been powered manually, by water, and finally by electricity.

Hundreds of aging original Mormon pioneers, among those who founded Salt Lake City, sat for this photograph on July 24, 1897, while in town to celebrate the Utah Pioneer Jubilee, commemorating the 50th anniversary of the city's founding.

Taken from a double-photo "stereocard" (used in dual magnifying glass viewers of the nineteenth century), this image captures the parade of surviving members of the Handcart Company, marching during the Pioneer Jubilee in Salt Lake City in July 1897. Unable to afford enough ox teams and wagons for Latter-day Saints immigrating to the Utah Territory, the Church provided some 650 carts that could be pulled by hand. Nearly 3,000 believers made the trip from Iowa City, Iowa, this way between 1856 and 1860.

Heber M. Wells (left), the first governor of Utah (1896–1905), waits in the rear of an open carriage with a man identified as Admiral Schley (in top hat, right), in front of the Wallace house at 5 Laurel Street on May 30, 1899. This is almost certainly Winfield Scott Schley, who destroyed the remnants of the Spanish fleet as it fled Santiago Bay on July 4, 1898, during the Spanish-American War. Given the May 30 date, he was probably in town for a Decoration Day (Memorial Day) event.

Street paving work (background) is under way to cover the carriage track–worn, dirt surface of South Temple Street, east of Main Street, in 1902. Buildings along the boulevard included the Alta Club, the Gardo House, and Amelia's Palace.

The majestic, cathedral-like Salt Lake City and County Building as it stood in 1902, from the southwest, between the 400 and 500 blocks of South, between State Street and 200 East (today, at 451 S. State Street). Reportedly, it was constructed to rival the Temple's magnificence during a period of tension between Mormon and non-Mormon residents.

Delivery coaches owned by merchant members of the Zion's Cooperative Mercantile Institution line up outside the department store to deliver goods to customers' homes around 1902.

City workers inspect a maze of crisscrossing streetcar tracks during road construction and paving at the intersection of Main Street and South Temple Street in 1902.

During a road improvement project at the intersection of South Temple and State Street in 1903, a man walks with a cane beneath the historic Eagle Gate monument, built by Brigham Young in 1859. The Bransford Apartments building is at right.

Men pose in front of the Zion's Cooperative Mercantile Institution's window. The sign proclaims "Holiness for the Lord." Religion permeated every aspect of community life including commerce in Salt Lake City's early history, which ultimately led to growing tension as increasing numbers of non-Mormons settled there.

A newsboy hawks papers while another lad sells American ice cream from a cart on bustling Commercial Street (34 East, between 100 and 200 South), which included the American Hotel (baths 15 cents) and Restaurant, the Palace Cafe, Johnson's Tavern (right side, halfway down the block), and Yee Lee's Laundry. A sign in the alley proclaims, "The New Devil is Coming."

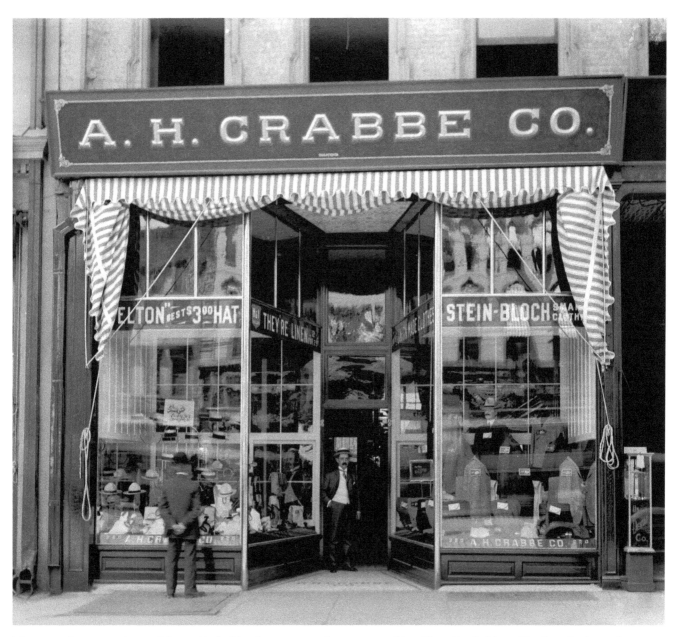

The Main Street storefront of the A. H. Crabbe Company men's store, owned by Albert H. Crabbe, offers hats for $3 in this photograph dated June 5, 1905. The Union Dental Company was up the stairs to the right. In 1916, Crabbe became chairman of the Salt Lake County Commission.

The six-story Commercial Block building dominates the corner at 76 West, 200 South, on June 19, 1905, fifteen years after its construction. Tenants included the New York Life Insurance agency, attorneys, at least two dentists (Peake and Barnett), and an aurist (ear specialist) named Dr. Arthur Douglas.

Employees line the front of the Century Printing Company shop at 167 West Temple Street on November 22, 1905.

A complex of electric lines converge near the Alta Club building, at the intersection of State Street and South Temple, on December 4, 1905. Founded in 1883, its initial members primarily came from the mining industry, but it drew industrial, financial, and social leaders from around the West. The building underwent a $4.2 million restoration early in the twenty-first century. The building in the background is the University Club.

A sign warns "Beware of Pickpockets" during the spring General Conference on Temple Square, at 50 West South Temple near the Bureau of Information Office.

Men and youths band together to witness a historic occasion—placement of the final streetcar pole to complete the citywide electric transit system, at the intersection of Main Street and 200 South, near the Walker Brothers Bank Building (at center), Park's Jewelry Store (center right), and the Scott Building (right).

In the midst of a clothing drive for the refugees of the April 18 earthquake that destroyed much of San Francisco, California, a crowd of men gathered on the sidewalk between the Herald Building and three trucks owned by the Redman Van and Storage Company on Main Street between 100 South and 200 South, April 26, 1906. The Redman company burned down in 1907 and later relocated to 400 West, where it added a fireproof storage facility.

New Buildings, New Streets, New Faces

(1906–1919)

Men in suits and women in white dresses and broad-brimmed hats stand at the 400 block of Main Street to view a parade (likely for the Fourth of July, given the flag-style bunting on the building).

This image was recorded from another spot during the same parade, showing the lengths to which some spectators would go—such as a dangerous climb to the top of a utility pole—to watch the parade down Main Street. Others parked their horses and buggies right beside the parade route to sit in or stand on.

A horse team is hitched to a wagon carrying an Adams Electric Drill, sold by the Salt Lake Hardware Company, at 42-52 West 200 South, May 17, 1906.

A bicyclist in shorts and a man in a suit and hat, astride a motor-powered bike, pose at the Salt Palace on 900 South, between Main and State streets, July 16, 1906.

Patches of snow cover the ground in this bird's-eye view of Salt Lake City, recorded in 1907 from on top of the City and County Building, between 400 and 500 South and State Street and 200 East.

People wait at the corner to cross while streetcars drive by during a busy day on Main Street, north of 200 South, about 1907. The tall Scott Building to the left housed the King Hardware and Stove Company. Smith Drug stands at the right corner, with signs down the street for the Salt Lake City car agent, the American Shoe Shine Parlor, and Meredith's Trunks.

The Davis Shoe Company, advertising "Money Back Shoes," attracted a large crowd for Buster Brown brand footwear at 236 South Main Street, on May 17, 1907. To the right is the J. H. Leyson Company jewelry store.

Small carriages line the north side of 200 South Street, west of Main Street, in 1907. A banner on the Cullen Hotel at left announces a complete remodeling has been completed. The hotel stands between the Chesapeake Cafe (foreground) and a billiards hall. The wagon in front of Chesapeake Cafe belongs to John Holley & Company, a wholesaler of butter, eggs, cheese, and poultry, who was probably making a delivery to the cafe.

Men working for Patrick (P. J.) Moran, a contractor, remove old cobblestones and paving while reconstructing streetcar rails at the intersection of Main Street and 200 South in 1907.

The interior framing of the Boston and Newhouse buildings is shown here during the simultaneous construction of the twin structures at the intersection of Exchange Place and Main Street, between 300 South and 400 South, on March 14, 1908.

Men and boys stand on a downtown cobblestone street to watch a man behind the wheel of a single-seat Studebaker car, apparently used for racing, on August 7, 1908.

This bird's-eye shot from atop the City and County Building shows Washington Square, the Boston and Newhouse buildings, and Temple Square in 1908. The triple-arch entrance to the Elite Theatre stands in the center foreground. A sign for I X L Furniture Company on the newly constructed P. A. Sorensen building (center) advertises, "You furnish the girl, we'll furnish the house."

The intersection of Main Street and 300 South, to the northwest, as it looked during a street-paving project in 1908.

An early automobile, decorated to serve as a float promoting the phonograph store during the United Commercial Travelers of America parade, sits at 327-329 Main Street on June 18, 1908. Featured on the car is a gramophone, complete with morning glory audio system.

Main Street to the north is shown from the roof of the Boston Building in 1908.

Workers from the Hamlin Paint Company give the facade of the Castle Hall Building at 261 South Main Street a new paint job on October 17, 1908. Madam Elon Lavera Snyder, "The Gifted Palmist, Psychic, and Card Reader," advertises her services on a large sign near several smaller ones for doctors.

Slats of wood protrude over the sidewalk, amid makeshift advertising signs, during construction of the Lyceum Theater at 271 25th Street, on January 9, 1909. The poster to the left advertises a play that opened in the city the previous month, on December 20.

The Colonial Theatre, 144 West 100 South Street, beside B. F. Ott Drug Company, proudly announced a matinee performance of "Shore Acres," starring Archie Boyd on February 6, 1909. Billed as "The Greatest Ladies and Childrens Play Ever Written," the popular show was in its 15th year on the American stage. The Will Rees Plumbing Company was installing heating and plumbing in the building, just the thing for a cold and snowy day.

Road builders, employed by contractor Patrick "P. J." Moran, remove original cobblestones while paving the east side of Main Street, north of 200 South, outside the Tribune Building, about 1909.

Workers pose beside a line of horse-drawn delivery wagons at the ready outside the American Linen Supply at 130-138 West 100 South on February 20, 1909.

The Hotel Bungalow–Bungalow Theatre building, 251 South State Street offered patrons both an evening of entertainment and a place to stay overnight, April 14, 1909. *La Tosca*, advertised on the rooftop marquee, may have been the touring play or the French movie version starring Sarah Bernhardt, which was released that year.

Sawhorses line the center of Main Street, south of Temple, during another paving project by P. J. Moran, outside the Zion's Cooperative Mercantile Institution (at left), about 1909. The Salt Lake Security and Trust Company and the Constitution Building are also pictured. The city was in the midst of an extensive effort to macadamize its streets and plant "parks" in the medians.

A sign advertising Cuban cigars fronts the College Inn and Cafe, 237 Main Street, on April 21, 1909. At left is the Utah Savings and Trust Company, and at right, Reagan's Bar and the Delmar Lunch Room.

A steamroller rumbles along the curb of Main Street, north of 300 South, with streetcars in the distance about 1909. Among the structures pictured are the Scott Building and the McCornick Block.

Dozens of young military cadets gather outside the Y.M.C.A. Building (center) during the Commercial Club's building campaign, at the southeast corner intersection of 100 South and State streets, May 12, 1909. The Utah Independent Telephone Company building is at left.

A large throng showed up to watch a crane lower the cornerstone of the new Commercial Club Building at 34 Exchange Place on July 5, 1909. The image also shows parts of the Boston Building (center) and post office (in background, with flags, right).

Streetcar tracks and overhead electrical lines lead to the Oregon Short Line Railroad Depot, which was still under construction when this photograph was taken on July 29, 1909, at the west end of South Temple, 300 West (today at 400 West). The line was part of the Union Pacific Railroad. Its galvanized iron cornice and roofing were manufactured by J. A. Johnson of Salt Lake City.

Building contractor P. J. Moran's crew removes cobblestones onto wagons during street reconstruction and paving on the west side of Main Street and 200 South, about 1909.

Paving projects in downtown Salt Lake City were done to facilitate the emerging automobile, like this classic model parked outside D. J. Watts' barbershop at 17 West South Temple, on July 31, 1909.

Sword-wielding high school students front a musical band of their fellow cadets during a parade down Main Street, south of 200 South, on August 24, 1909.

Two horses, one hitched to a delivery wagon, wait outside the Clayton-Daynes Music Company, which sold a variety of instruments, large and small, as well as phonographs, at 17 West South Temple on September 23, 1909.

A row of soldiers and an officer stand at attention opposite a group of bystanders, in anticipation of a parade marking a visit by President William Howard Taft on September 25, 1909.

Automobile passengers pose in front of the Colonial Theatre at 144 West 100 South, which was presenting the popular musical comedy play *The Time, the Place, and the Girl*, on November 7, 1909. When the play was made into a movie 20 years later, it starred Betty Compson of Beaver, Utah, who attended high school in Salt Lake City.

The three-story Clift House hotel shared its location at 280 South Main Street with the Red Cross Dentist and the Van Dyke Drug Company, November 27, 1909.

Rows of carriages stand inside the corridor between the twin modern buildings, Boston (left) and Newhouse (right), facing east on Exchange Place, September 30, 1909.

A bicycle is parked in front of the Intermountain Electric Company, between horse-drawn vehicles at 13 South Main Street, on November 6, 1909. Cannon Brothers Architects and Engineers were upstairs. Next door on the left, at Number 11, was the George Q. Cannon Association, Real Estate and Brokerage ("We sell the Earth").

The Lion House (center), beside the Beehive House (left), owned by the Church of Jesus Christ of Latter-day Saints, between Main Street and State Street, south of Temple, about 1910.

Horses and wagons stand in the main business district of the mining town of Bingham, Utah, a few miles southwest of Salt Lake City, about 1910. The town was consumed by expanded mining operations in the 1970s.

A rider, with umbrella, sits inside a stationary buggy on Salt Lake City's Main Street about 1910.

Three horses were needed to pull a wagon used by the Redman Van & Storage Company at 113-117 South West Temple in 1910. Its advertising slogan, "It's your move," was cleverly painted on a pattern resembling a chess board. The three-digit phone number is conspicuous; today, 555 is the standard telephone prefix used in films and television shows, because it isn't assigned within the United States.

Early electric-powered automobiles of the Taxicab and Automobile Company, with uniformed drivers, were ready for hire (by way of telephone number 1598) on January 25, 1910. The location was Eagle Block, between 200 and 300 South, West Temple, shared by Crismon & Nichols Assayers, the Big 4 Advertising Company, and an enormous building ad painted by the Utah Billposting Company, touting Henry George brand 5-cent cigars.

A group of men and a boy in a cap pose with a Buick from the Randall-Dodd Auto Company, outside 229 South Main Street, where William A. Stickney Cigar Company and Hulbert Brothers Trunk Manufacturers were located, February 21, 1910.

Main Street, north of 200 South, with the Herald Building and the McCornick Block, about 1910. Businesses included Mehesy Furs (at left-center), Margells Brothers Toys, Books and Stationery (penultimate building on the left), and Salt Lake Medical (right center), as well as street vendors' carts.

A right-side driver with a youngster sit inside a Buick car aimed toward the camera outside the Randall-Dodd Auto Company, 231 South State Street, on April 14, 1910. The cross on the grill may have been part of a promotion for the Red Cross organization or for the city's Red Cross Drugstore.

Three men pause while working to convert an automobile into a vehicle to carry small groups of tourists, April 17, 1910.

Telephone and streetcar lines and poles run end-to-end through this general shot of 200 South, west of Main Street, also known as Commercial Block, about 1910. A sign on the corner building informs passersby that J. P. Paulson of 170 & 174 "W. 2nd S. St." provided the fixtures used in that bank.

White-capped, uniformed union members prepare to walk in the annual Labor Day Parade, September 5, 1910.

Flowers, ice cream, fruits, toiletries, and cut-rate drugs were among wares available at Brice's State Pharmacy, a corner store at 18 South Main Street, on October 21, 1910.

With aviation still in its infancy, onlookers at Saltair, a resort in Salt Lake County, stand to watch a demonstration of aircraft, as an automobile (right) whizzes by, April 6, 1911.

During the Salt Lake City *Tribune's* "Buy a paper to support the Humane Society fund" promotion, some actors and actresses helped sell papers in front of the Tribune Building, on Progress Block, 141-153 South Main Street, about 1911. Humane societies in that era generally aided needy, often orphaned, children, rather than animals.

In this promotional photograph taken on May 28, 1911, men sit on early-model motorcycles at the Bicycle Supply Company, 64 West 300 South, which is advertising an upcoming race at the Salt Palace. Two other businesses in the image are the Hubbard Investment Company (at left) and H. E. Giers and Company (selling furniture, at right).

Burros are employed to hold signs advertising the Alford Brothers Company, a clothing store at 15 West 200 South, on August 11, 1911. A man dressed as a mining prospector (center) apparently is meant to accompany the animals. Each sign contains the motto, "Go West Young Man," popularized by the nineteenth-century journalist Horace Greeley, publisher of the New York *Tribune*.

A manned balloon floats over this scene of Main Street, which includes the White House Hotel, at right, on the block of 200 South, September 6, 1911.

The Star Bargain store attracts lines of customers for its "Fire, Smoke and Water Sale" of clothing held inside Daniel's Theatre at 253 South State Street, September 7, 1911.

President William Howard Taft, on a platform decorated with flags and plants, gestures during an address at the Utah State Fair Grounds during an official visit on October 5, 1911. Taft served one term, from 1909 to 1913.

A crowd of men wait for the doors to open outside the A. H. Crabbe men's clothing store, at 220 South Main Street, on Harkins Block, on May 11, 1912, during a sale to raise $15,000 in fifteen days. Three newsboys (foreground) apparently were taking the opportunity to sell papers.

The University of Utah men's baseball team and its managers pose with grandstands behind them, on the home field on the east end of 200 South at Presidents Circle (1400 East), May 23, 1912.

On Pioneer Day, July 24, 1912, honoring the original Mormon pioneers who settled Salt Lake City in 1847, the Armour and Company meat store used vines and bunting to decorate its horse-pulled float for the upcoming parade, shown here at Liberty Park (currently 922 South 700 East).

Covered cars from the Campbell Auto Company form a procession at Liberty Park along the crowded route of the Pioneer Day parade, on July 24, 1912.

Two men in a packed auto stopped in Salt Lake City at the Bertram Motor Supply Company, 249-251 South State Street, on September 21, 1912, while on a marathon drive from San Francisco to New York City promoting the future Panama-Pacific Exposition.

The Republican Party festooned its headquarters at the Merchants Bank building, 227 Main Street, with American flags and fabric decorations, October 2, 1912, in preparation for the upcoming presidential election. Their man, incumbent William Howard Taft, who had visited Salt Lake City the year before, lost to Democrat Woodrow Wilson after former president Teddy Roosevelt entered the race on a separate ticket and split the Republican vote.

The arrowhead-shaped arch of the Eagle Gate Monument (left) is seen beside the Bransford Apartment House and intersecting streetcar power lines at South Temple and State Street, October 21, 1912. Eagle Gate was first built in 1859 to mark the entrance to Brigham Young's property at the mouth of City Creek Canyon. It has been replaced several times.

Large rooftop signs on the Auerbach Building tout the multi-floored department store on the northeast corner of State Street and Broadway as "Utah's Most Popular," November 16, 1912.

Dental services and men's clothes were available on the second floor of the Walker Brothers Bank Building at 200 South and Main Street, November 22, 1912.

Horses drag a plow owned by the Cooperative Wagon and Machine Company while grading a strip of ground in Salt Lake County, as adults, children, and their pets look on, May 20, 1913. The grading may have been for extension of the Bamberger Intercity Railway, which renamed this area Cleverly Crossing in 1920.

In Sandy (now a Salt Lake City suburb), residents stand outside the Oldham and Powell Company store below a sign that advertises the Bywater Fire Extinguisher and Fire Department Supply Company and welcomes visiting union firemen, August 21, 1913.

On Capitol Hill at the Utah State Capitol, dignitaries pose amid American flags during a ceremony marking the laying of the statehouse building's cornerstone, on April 4, 1914. Salt Lake City has always been Utah's territorial and state capital, with the exception of 1851–56, when the town of Fillmore was the legal capital.

Park's Jewelry Store, with its rooftop and painted building signs, was the main tenant of the five-story Boyd Park Building (center), at 170 South Main Street, September 21, 1914.

Street resurfacing by contractor P. J. Moran on Main Street doesn't seem to stop activity among streetcars, automobiles, and wagons at 200 South and Main. This bird's-eye view includes the corner high-rise Walker Brothers Bank Building at 175 Main Street, about 1914.

Scaffolding and construction cranes jut out beside the planned rotunda during construction of the Utah State Capitol, January 15, 1915.

Men pose inside automobiles in a promotional picture for the Bettilyon Home Builders Company, at 340-342 Main Street, on March 19, 1915.

An "Official Guide Post Truck" owned by the B. F. Goodrich tire company is parked by the firm's Salt Lake City location, 128 South State Street, next to two men astride an early motorcycle, on September 15, 1915.

Snowfall provides a scenic, late-winter view of the Salt Lake City and County Building, between 400 and 500 South, on March 24, 1916.

A temporary archway, known as the No-Ni-Shee Arch, was built near the intersection of Main and South Temple streets for the Wizard of the Wasatch celebration, September 21, 1916. The arch was dedicated to No-Ni-Shee, the name of a mythical Native American "salt princess," whose salt-filled tears were believed to have made the Great Salt Lake. During the 1916 celebration, saltwater was sprayed on the arch and it later crystallized on Main Street.

Joseph Simons, a grocer, stands next to a Kelly-Springfield delivery truck, filled with hay bales outside the 10th Ward cash grocery, hay, grain, and coal store, 424 South East, on January 19, 1917.

Two men in business suits stand next to a delivery truck for the Clover Dairy, near the New York Building, on what was Post Office Park (present-day Market Street), at 340 South, between Main and Temple streets, May 27, 1917. The Boston Building is visible in the distance (center right).

Amid thick drifts of snow, a large shipment of bicycles in narrow boxes sits outside the Charles A. Fowler store at 112 West 200 South on January 17, 1918. The photograph also shows other businesses in the building to the right: the Utah Machinery Company, Lodge Pool Room, and Eber W. Hall Undertaker, Funeral Director and Embalmer.

An auto traffic light pole fits into the center of intersecting street rail tracks outside the Auerbach Building, on the northeast corner of State Street and Broadway, May 11, 1918.

Automobiles show a greater presence downtown in this shot of 200 South, east from West Temple toward Main Street, recorded on May 11, 1918. An Orpheum Theater sign (renamed the Capitol Theater in 1927) is visible at right, and farther down the street is the Walker Brothers Bank Building.

This group of young boys posed for a photograph on an early model bus near the Gardner and Adams Company's store, at 138-140 South Main Street, July 22, 1918.

General John J. "Black Jack" Pershing, the venerated commander-in-chief of the U.S. Army Expeditionary Force during World War I, stands (facing camera) inside a flag-draped automobile as a crowd watches in front of the Utah Hotel at 15 East South Temple, on January 16, 1920. At the time, Pershing (1860–1948), was still in service. Congress named him General of the Armies, a permanent rank previously accorded only to George Washington, and that posthumously.

Stalled by the Great Depression

(1920–1939)

The Utah State Capitol can be seen in the distance in this view of State Street to the north, February 16, 1920.

A circus sideshow, with various animal acts and a pair of carnival barkers on podiums, stands ready for paying customers, in the area north of 400 South, on April 26, 1920.

The Rogers Amusement Company put on a carnival, with a small Ferris wheel and sideshow (background left) north of 400 South, east of State Street, April 28, 1920. The City and County Building is in view at far-left. One booth advertises J. G. McDonald chocolates, while another—not yet completed—promotes the American Legion organization representing military veterans. Salt Lake City's Service Star Legion (also called the War Mothers) was the first of the SSL groups in America. They improved and supported Memory Grove Park and Memorial House.

With flags hanging over his head, President Woodrow Wilson, tipping his hat to onlookers, stands inside an open car in a parade given in his honor downtown about 1920. Wilson served as president from 1913 to 1921.

A crowd gathers to watch a devastating fire that swept through a stadium grandstand in Salt Lake City about 1920.

The newly built Keith O'Brien Building, with a distinctive sign bearing the owner's initials, rules over both sides of the southwest corner of State Street and 300 South, June 10, 1920.

The soda fountain and well-stocked shelves and display counters, some with cutout advertisements, inside the 6th Avenue drugstore at 402 6th Street, August 27, 1920. Above the candy counter (right background), a Sweets Salt Lake Chocolates ad hangs beside one for Cracker Jacks.

Proud workers pose with boxes of products piled to capacity on this truck, owned by the Berriju Company, at 152-154 East South Street, on May 21, 1921.

Workers stand at the soda fountain inside of the Zion's Cooperative Mercantile Institution at 15 South Main Street in the 1920s. By then, the department store was almost half a century old.

The proprietor of Lingo's Grocery, specializing in Greek-style food, at 126 West and 2nd south, about 1930.

Buses—or "stages" as they were still called—are parked outside and in the terminal of the Pickwick Stages System. Mechanics stand lined up at left and uniformed drivers at right, with what appear to be managers and office staff, at 27 North West Temple, about 1931.

Salt Lake City's minor league baseball team (in white uniforms, left) lines the first base side of their home field, opposite the team from Boise, Idaho, about 1935. An announcer is sitting in a box hanging over the grandstands, which are full of spectators.

On a snow-covered Temple Square stands the Mormon Tabernacle auditorium, with its board dome, as it appeared in this northwesterly view on February 20, 1937.

Suburban Growth and Presidential Visits

(1940–1950s)

With the Utah State Capitol as an appropriate backdrop, members of the Utah State Highway Patrol's motorcycle squad pose for this picture about 1940.

Automobiles parked in various positions cluster within the open market at 130-150 Pacific Avenue about 1940.

Discounted goods were to be found in the basement of the Zion's Cooperative Mercantile Institution on Main Street, shown here crowded with patrons in 1949.

The Fred A. Carleson Company, at 535 South Main Street, was a full-service auto center—new cars, used cars (right), and a Chevron gas and service station (left), June 17, 1949.

Twin towers frame the Holy Trinity Greek Church, beside the World War II memorial building at left, in the late 1940s.

President Harry S. Truman arrived in Salt Lake City in 1952 for a whistle-stop campaign visit to help the candidacy of Democratic Party presidential nominee Adlai Stevenson and running mate John J. Sparkman. Their Republican opponents, General Dwight Eisenhower and Richard Nixon, would win the election later that year.

Ab Jenkins, in a pith helmet, took a break from speeding cars on the Bonneville Salt Flats to officiate an Independence Day soapbox derby for local boys, July 4, 1951.

Notes on the Photographs

These notes, listed by page number, attempt to include all aspects known of the photographs. Each of the photographs is identified by the page number, a title or description, photographer and collection, archive, and call or box number when applicable. Although every attempt was made to collect all data, in some cases complete data may have been unavailable due to the age and condition of some of the photographs and records.

23 ALTA CLUB

24 CONFERENCE CROWD

25 THE LAST STREETCAR POLE

26 VANS IN FRONT OF HERALD BUILDING

28 MAIN STREET PARADE

29 PARADE

30 ADAMS ELECTRIC DRILL AT SALT LAKE HARDWARE

31 BICYCLE RIDER

32 BIRD'S-EYE VIEW OF SNOW-COVERED CITY

33 MAIN STREET

34 BUSTER BROWN CROWD

35 SOUTH STREET, 1907

36 RECONSTRUCTING THE RAILS

37 NEWHOUSE BUILDING

38 STUDEBAKER

39 BIRD'S-EYE VIEW, 1908

40 MAIN STREET AND 300 SOUTH

41 PHONOGRAPH COMPANY FLOAT WITH GRAMOPHONE

42 MAIN STREET, NORTH FROM BOSTON BUILDING

43 CASTLE HALL PAINT JOB

44 LYCEUM THEATRE

45 COLONIAL THEATRE

46 STREET PAVING

47 AMERICAN LINEN SUPPLY COMPANY WAGONS

48 BUNGALOW THEATRE

49 SAWHORSES ON MAIN

50 COLLEGE INN AND CAFE

51 STEAMROLLER AT THE CURB, 1909

52 MILITARY CADETS AT Y.M.C.A.

53 LAYING THE CORNERSTONE FOR COMMERCIAL CLUB

54 OREGON SHORT LINE DEPOT

55 REMOVING COBBLESTONES

56 D. J. WATTS BARBERSHOP

57 CADETS IN PARADE

58 CLAYTON-DAYNES MUSIC COMPANY

133

121 SALT LAKE AND
BOISE BALL CLUBS

122 TEMPLE SQUARE
Library of Congress
157858pu

124 STATE HIGHWAY
PATROL
MOTORCYCLES

125 OPEN MARKET AT
PACIFIC AVENUE,
1940

126 SHOPPERS AT ZION'S
COOPERATIVE
J. Willard Marriott
Library
University of Utah
p0838n01_03_17

127 FRED A. CARLESON
COMPANY AT SOUTH
MAIN

128 HOLY TRINITY GREEK
CHURCH
J. Willard Marriott
Library
University of Utah
p0121n01_06_03

129 HARRY TRUMAN
CAMPAIGNING, 1952

130 AB JENKINS AT
SOAPBOX DERBY